PlayTime® Pi

T0083294

Hymns

Level 1

5-Finger Melodies

Arranged by

Nancy and Randall Faber

Production: Frank and Gail Hackinson
Production Coordinators: Marilyn Cole
Cover: Terpstra Design, San Francisco
Music Editor: Edwin McLean
Engraving: Tempo Music Press, Inc.

FABER
PIANO ADVENTURES®

3042 Creek Drive
Ann Arbor, Michigan 48108

A NOTE TO TEACHERS

PlayTime® Piano Hymns is a collection of favorite hymns arranged for the Level 1 pianist. The arrangements use elementary 5-finger hand positions that reinforce note names & interval recognition. The selections offer excellent supplementary material and they are perfect for Sunday School and church performance.

PlayTime® Piano Hymns is part of the *PlayTime® Piano* series. "PlayTime" designates Level 1 of the *PreTime® to BigTime® Piano Supplementary Library* arranged by Faber and Faber.

Following are the levels of the supplementary library, which lead from *PreTime® to BigTime®.*

PreTime® Piano	(Primer Level)
PlayTime® Piano	(Level 1)
ShowTime® Piano	(Level 2A)
ChordTime® Piano	(Level 2B)
FunTime® Piano	(Level 3A – 3B)
BigTime® Piano	(Level 4)

Each level offers books in a variety of styles, making it possible for the teacher to offer stimulating material for every student. For a complimentary detailed listing, e-mail faber@pianoadventures.com or write us at the mailing address below.

Visit **www.PianoAdventures.com**.

Teacher Duets

Optional teacher duets are a valuable feature of **PlayTime® Hymns**. Although the arrangements stand complete on their own, they sound richer and fuller when played as duets. And not incidentally, they allow the opportunity for parent and student to play together.

Helpful Hints:

1. The student should know his or her part thoroughly—and be able to play his or her part up an octave—before the teacher duet is used. Accurate rhythm is especially important.

2. Harmony notes in the student part may be omitted if a steady rhythm is difficult to achieve.

3. Rehearsal numbers are provided to give the student and teacher starting places.

4. The teacher may wish to count softly a measure before beginning, as this will help the ensemble.

ISBN 978-1-61677-000-6

TABLE OF CONTENTS

Middle C Position

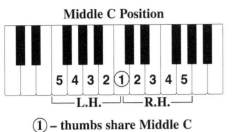

① – thumbs share Middle C

Jesus Loves Me

Text – Anna Warner
Tune – Wm. Bradbury

Happily

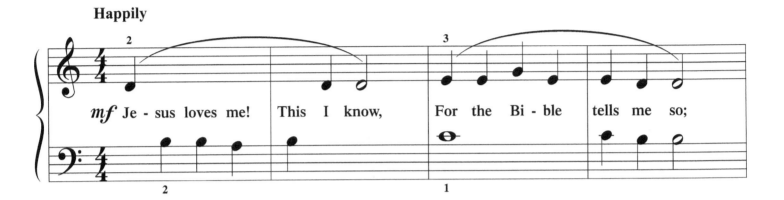

Je - sus loves me! This I know, For the Bi - ble tells me so;

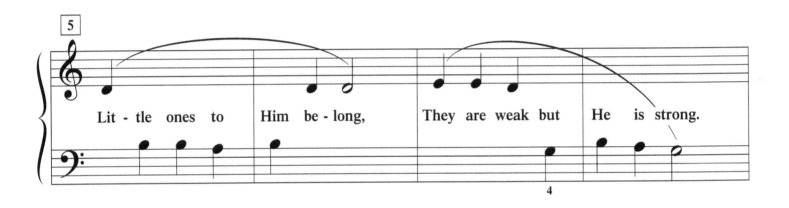

Lit - tle ones to Him be - long, They are weak but He is strong.

Teacher Duet: (Student plays 1 octave higher)

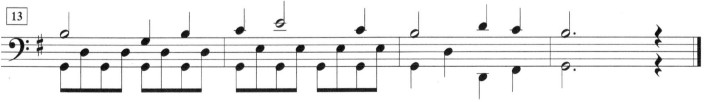

Do Lord

Text – Anonymous
Tune – Spiritual

Combining Middle C and C Positions

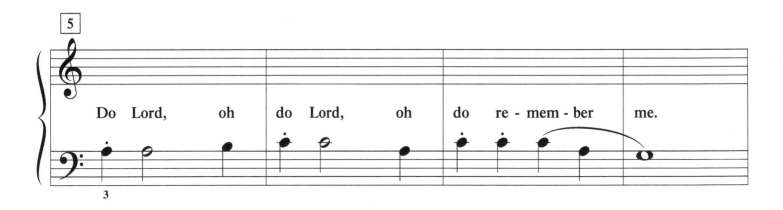

Teacher Duet: (Student plays 1 octave higher)

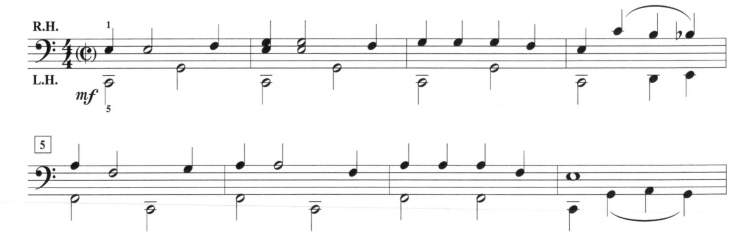

Do Lord, oh do Lord, oh do re - mem - ber me. Look a -

cresc.

Move L.H. to C Position

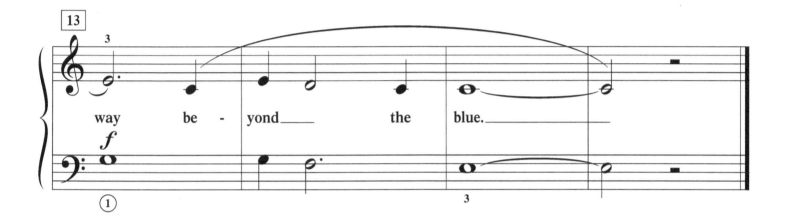

way be - yond____ the blue._____

cresc.

rit.

FF1000

Stand Up, Stand Up for Jesus

Text – George Duffield
Tune – George Webb

Combining Middle C and C Positions

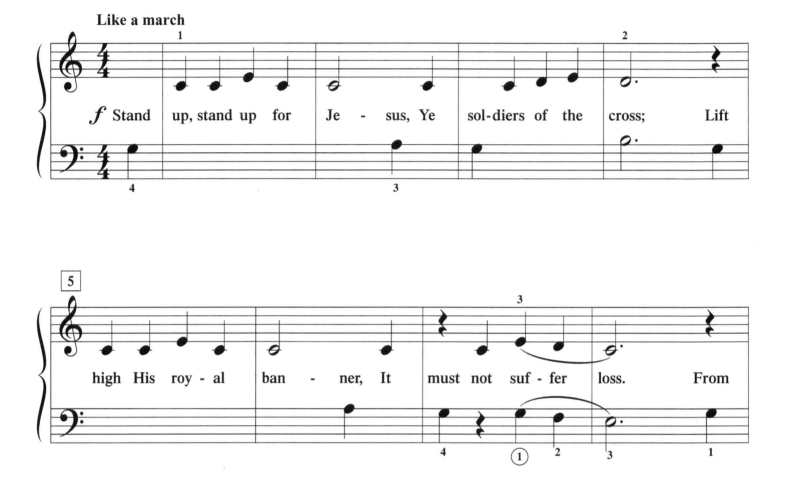

Teacher Duet: (Student plays 1 octave higher)

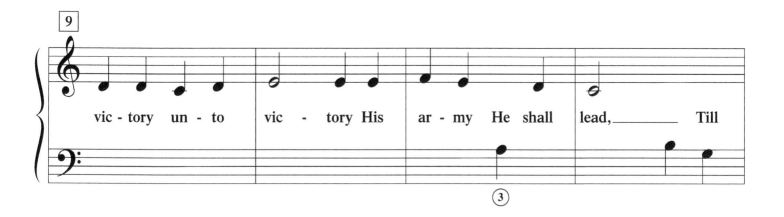

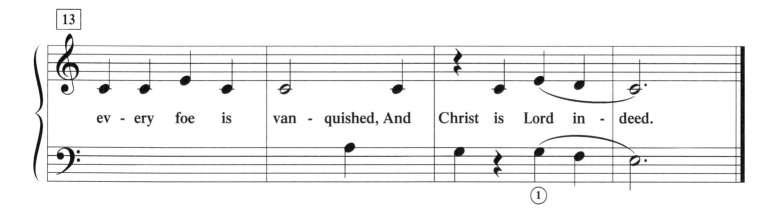

10

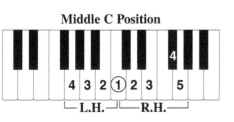

Holy, Holy, Holy

Text – Reginald Heber
Tune – John B. Dykes

With joy

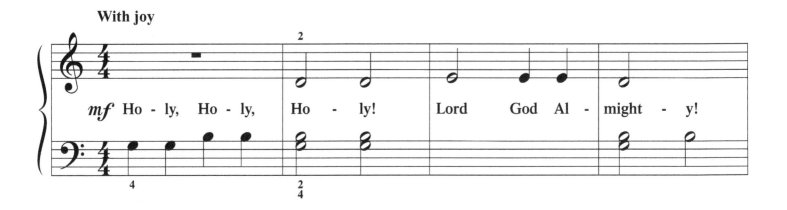

mf Ho - ly, Ho - ly, Ho - ly! Lord God Al - might - y!

Ear - ly in the morn - ing our song shall rise to Thee;

Teacher Duet: (Student plays 1 octave higher)

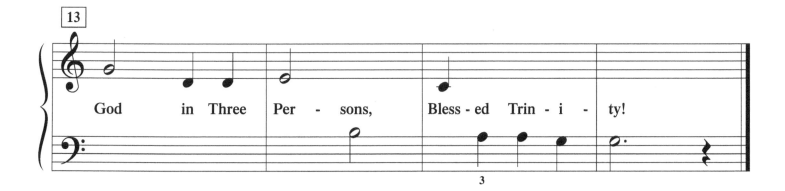

This Little Light of Mine

Text – Anonymous
Tune – Spiritual

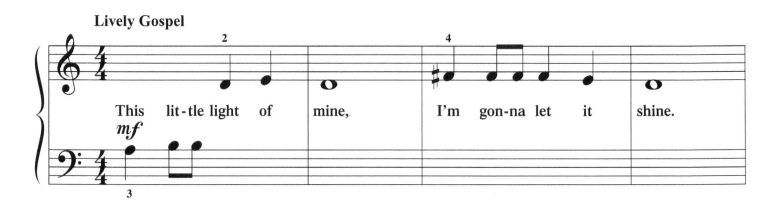

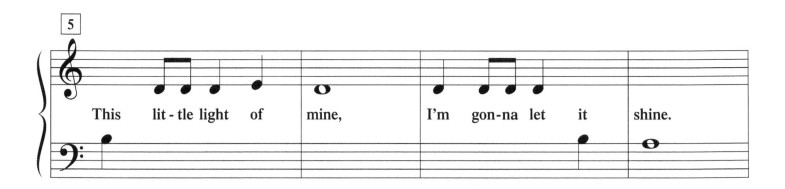

Teacher Duet: (Student plays 1 octave higher)

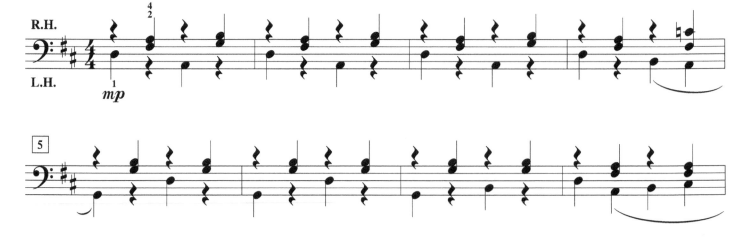

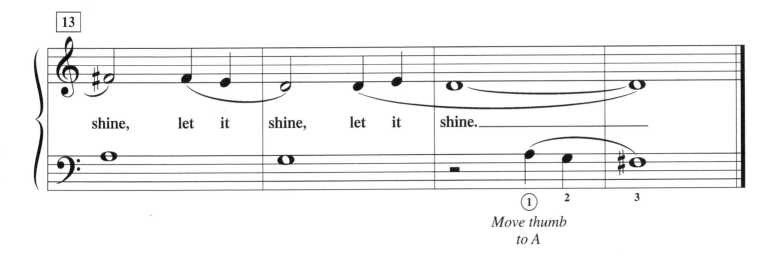

FF1000

14

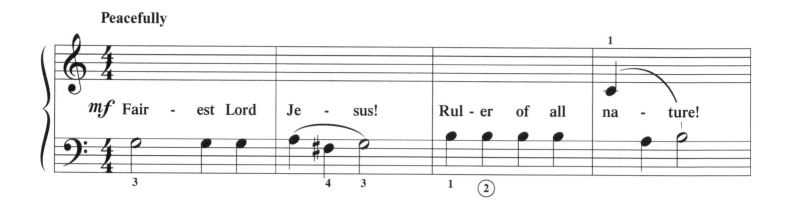

Fairest Lord Jesus

Text – Munster Gesangbuch
Tune – Silesian Folk Song

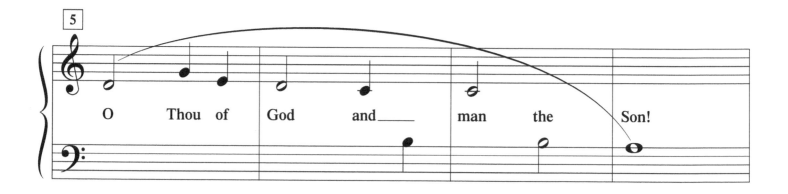

Teacher Duet: (Student plays 1 octave higher)

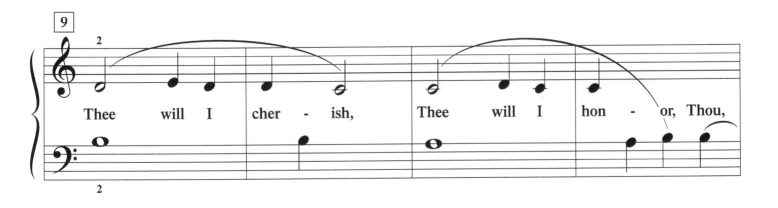

Thee will I cher - ish, Thee will I hon - or, Thou,

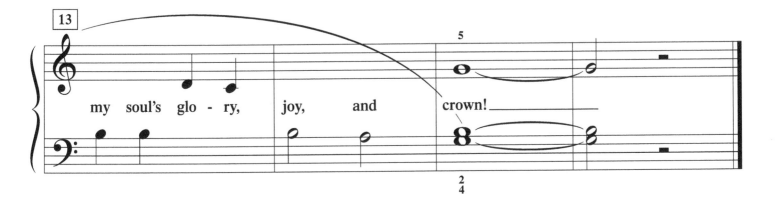

my soul's glo - ry, joy, and crown!

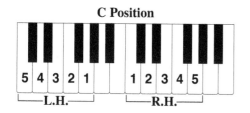

Joyful, Joyful
We Adore Thee

Text – Henry van Dyke
Tune – Ludwig van Beethoven

With enthusiasm

mf Joy - ful, joy - ful | we a - dore Thee, | God of glo - ry, | Lord of love;

Hearts un - fold like | flowers be - fore Thee, | Open - ing to the | sun a - bove.

Teacher Duet: (Student plays 2 octaves higher)

18

Middle C Position

O Worship the King

Text – Robert Grant
Tune – Johann Haydn

Not too fast

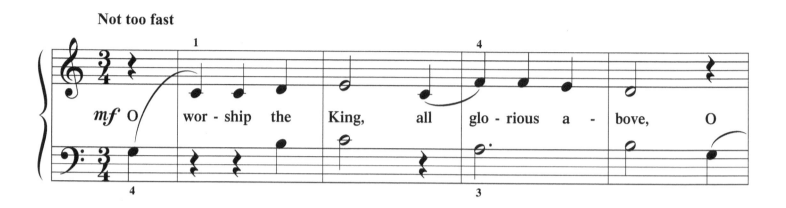

O wor - ship the King, all glo - rious a - bove, O

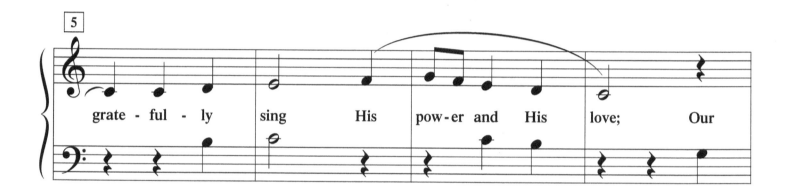

grate - ful - ly sing His pow-er and His love; Our

Teacher Duet: (Student plays 1 octave higher)

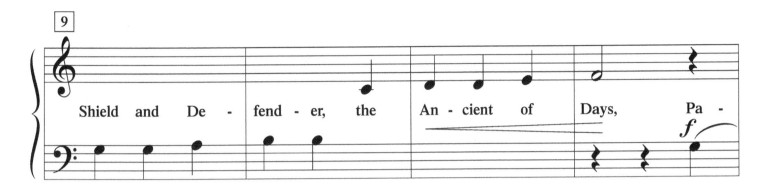

Shield and De - fend - er, the An - cient of Days, Pa -

vil - ioned in splen - dor and gird - ed with praise.

What a Friend
We Have in Jesus

Text – Joseph Scriven
Tune – Chas. Converse

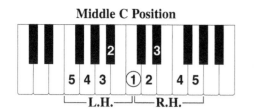

Sweetly

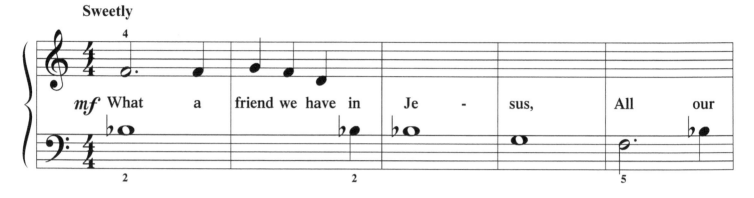

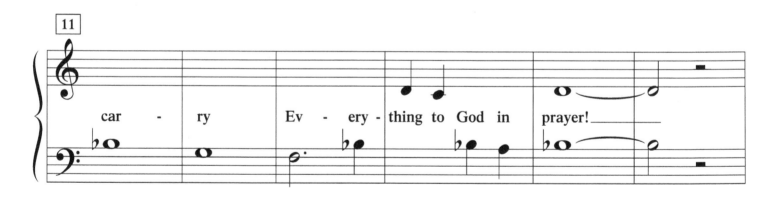

Teacher Duet: (Student plays 1 octave higher)

FF1000

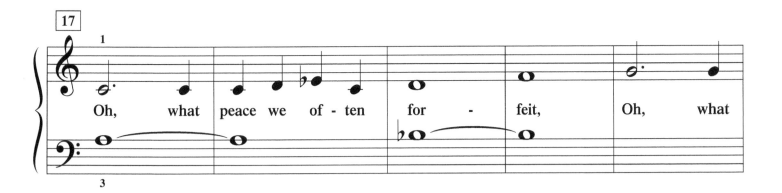

Oh, what peace we of - ten for - feit, Oh, what

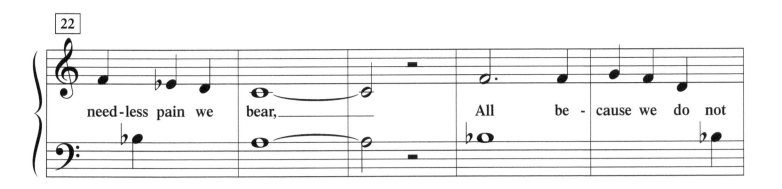

need-less pain we bear, All be - cause we do not

car - ry Ev - ery - thing to God in prayer.

Middle C Position

Come Thou Almighty King

Text – Anonymous
Tune – Felice de Giardini

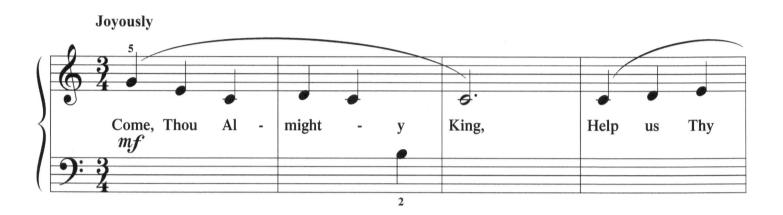

Joyously

Come, Thou Al - might - y King, Help us Thy

mf

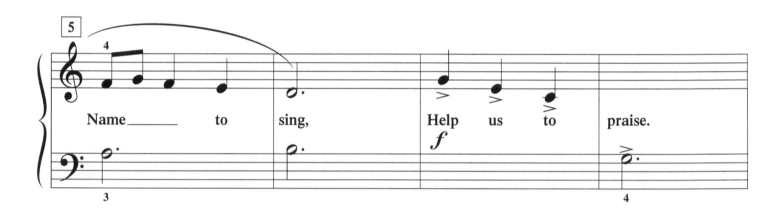

Name____ to sing, Help us to praise.

f

Teacher Duet: (Student plays 1 octave higher)

R.H.

mf

L.H.

f

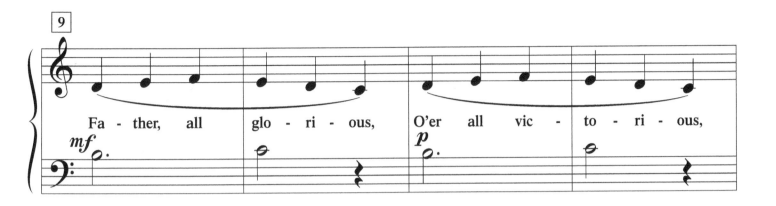

Fa - ther, all glo - ri - ous, O'er all vic - to - ri - ous,

mf   *p*

Come and reign o - ver us, An - cient of Days.

f

mp   *p*

mf

24

Middle C Position

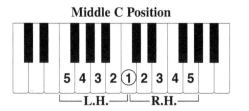

For the Beauty
of the Earth

Text – F. Pierpoint
Tune – Conrad Kocher

Cheerfully

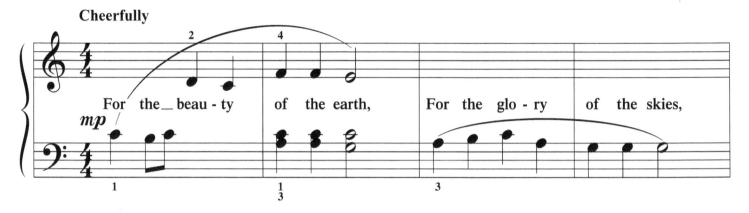

For the beau-ty of the earth, For the glo-ry of the skies,

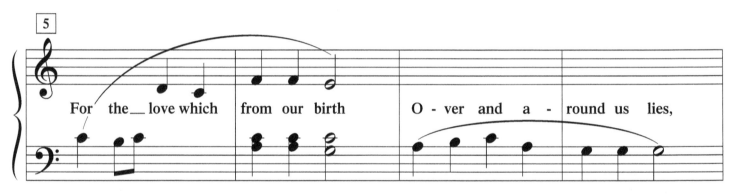

For the love which from our birth O-ver and a-round us lies,

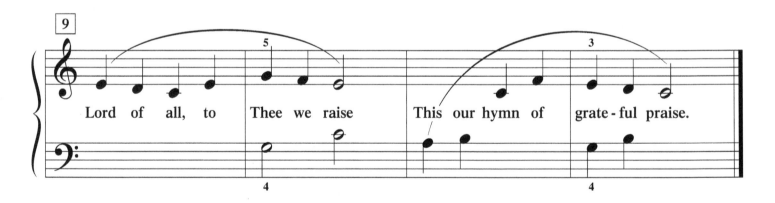

Lord of all, to Thee we raise This our hymn of grate-ful praise.

Teacher Duet: (Student plays 1 octave higher)

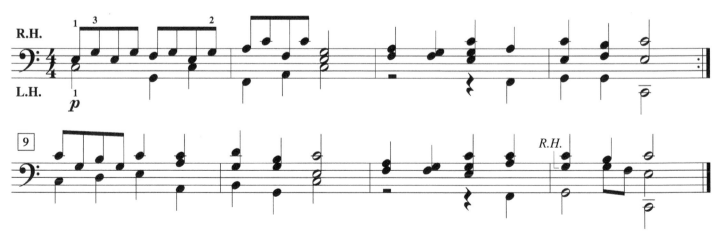